Crazy Creatures

Edited By Machaela Gavaghan

First published in Great Britain in 2019 by:

Young Writers
Remus House
Coltsfoot Drive
Peterborough
PE2 9BF
Telephone: 01733 890066
Website: www.youngwriters.co.uk

All Rights Reserved
Book Design by Ashley Janson
© Copyright Contributors 2019
Softback ISBN 978-1-83928-585-1

Printed and bound in the UK by BookPrintingUK
Website: www.bookprintinguk.com
YB0426K

FOREWORD

Hello Reader!

For our latest poetry competition we sent out funky and vibrant worksheets for primary school pupils to fill in and create their very own poem about fiendish fiends and crazy creatures. I got to read them and guess what? They were **roarsome**!

The pupils were able to read our example poems and use the fun-filled free resources to help bring their imaginations to life, and the result is pages **oozing** with exciting poetic tales. From friendly monsters to mean monsters, from bumps in the night to **rip-roaring** adventures, these pupils have excelled themselves, and now have the joy of seeing their work in print!

Here at Young Writers we love nothing more than poetry and creativity. We aim to encourage children to put pen to paper to inspire a love of the written word and explore their own unique worlds of creativity. We'd like to congratulate all of the aspiring authors that have created this book of **monstrous mayhem** and we know that these poems will be enjoyed for years to come. So, dive on in and submerge yourself in all things furry and fearsome (and perhaps check under the bed!).

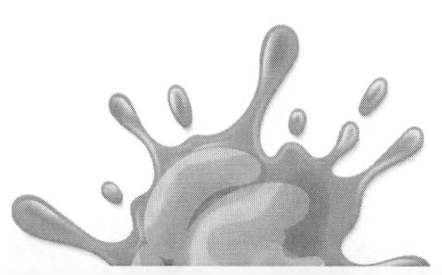
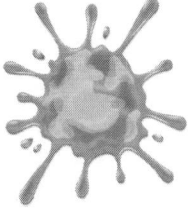

CONTENTS

Andalusia Academy, St Matthias Park

Amina Torofdar (10)	1
Aisha Nounu (8)	2
Sumaya Saeed Awil (10)	3
Saifullah Ahmed Safdar (10)	4
Aisha Sumaya Ahmed (10)	5
Mumtaz Yoonis (9)	6
Azhaan Nadeem (9)	7
Arhum Haroon (10)	8
Reye Mohamed Saad (10)	9
Saarah Hamid (8)	10

Argyle House School, Tunstall Road

Elyssa Stoker (10)	11
Lily Grace Mileham (7)	12
Joseph Allan Wheatley (8)	13
Aneesha Kaur (9)	14
Molly Lancaster (7)	15
Holly Quinn (8)	16
Ellie Calvert (9)	17
Grace Urwin (8)	18
Yara Abouleid (8)	19
Aryan Batth (9)	20
Ajumoke Amy-Jean Maughan (8)	21
Elliot Fallows George Paxton (9)	22
Oliver Hunter (9)	23
Brooke Frances Hunter (7)	24
Henry Hutchinson-Khan (8)	25
Nathan Smith (11)	26
Summer Lily Marshall-Graham (7)	27
Jasmin Kaur (7)	28

Oscar Smiles (8)	29

Birdham CE Primary School, Birdham

Bronwyn Holden (8)	30
Fraizer Golds (8)	31
Amy Leigh Tebbs (8)	32
Niamh Munnery (8)	33
Lillie Lowery (9)	34
Ava Richards (8)	35
Florence Wilson (8)	36
George Sheperd (8)	37
Darcey Louise Nunn Knowles (9)	38
Marcus Irvine-Smith (8)	39
Joshua Ellis (8)	40
Fallon Cole (8)	41
Bertie Jones (8)	42
Max Sargent (9)	43
Dexter Drew (8)	44
Ernie Livings (10)	45
Beau Madden (8)	46
Thomas Bacon (9)	47
Raf Kennedy (8)	48
Fynn Cornwell (8)	49
Charlie Graham Ashdown (8)	50
Edward Palmer-Felgate (8)	51
Zia Mahmood-Jones (8)	52
Joe Tranchant (8)	53

Hillside Academy, Denaby Main

Kayla-May Palmer (9)	54
Alicia Murray (10)	55
Jessica Lockett (9)	56
Millie Cooper (9)	57

Cody Dodd (9) — 58
Denver Leigh Mathieson (9) — 59

Jessop Primary School, Herne Hill

Jasiah McDermott (8) — 60
Francisco Jackson (5) — 61

St Christophers Academy, Dunstable

Caroline Morgans (7) — 62
Macey Joseph (7) — 64
Zaynab Sheikh (7) — 65
Oliver Woodall (7) — 66
Theo Kiely (8) — 68
Tom McCarthy (7) — 69
Jacob Jojo (7) — 70
Bright Onunwa (7) — 71
Inaaya Ahmed (7) — 72
Pallavi Pandya (7) — 73
Felix Owen Davies (8) — 74
Jessica Bell-Cooper (7) — 75
Franek Kloza (7) — 76
Jasmine Dhesi (7) — 77
Samantha Nnadozie (7) — 78
Grace Daniels (7) — 79
Ellie Cook (7) — 80
Farhaan Ali Sarwar (7) — 81
William Kimberley (7) — 82
Mia Rose (7) — 83
George Kimberley (7) — 84
Surayya Dauhoo (8) — 85
Riley Battams (7) — 86

St Peter's CE Middle School, Old Windsor

Ava Jessica Peppiatt (10) — 87
Rocco Valentine Eastell (10) — 88
Maisy Eva Wood (10) — 89
Isabella Katherine Ann Spurling (10) — 90
Honeysuckle Moon Morris (10) — 91

Sirut Kaur Hayre (10) — 92
Josie Clarke (10) — 93
Ella Louise Taylor (10) — 94
Sohana Jhanji (10) — 95
Charlotte Stoner (10) — 96
Sophie Harrap (10) — 97
Cailley Bristow (10) — 98
Annabel Crilly-McKean — 99
Matthew Newell (11) — 100
Tilly Wright (10) — 101
Phoebe Farmer (10) — 102
Elliot Whitehorn (10) — 103
Redmond Barron-Cheeseman (10) — 104
Avarni Kaur Purewal (11) — 105
Kayla Whitehead (10) — 106
May Hollick (10) — 107
Leya Oulahsein (10) — 108
Oskar Edward Thompson Totten (10) — 109

Wood Farm Primary School, Headington

Klaudia Stawinska (9) — 110
Kai Davies (10) — 112
Merlin Monson (9) — 114
Hamdi Guled Hasan (9) — 115
Narges Shafayi (9) — 116
Shania Darcey Lewis (10) — 117
Senara Bambaravanage (10) — 118
Samrah Hirah Shah (11) — 119
Kacper Jakub Mackowski (9) — 120
Cyrus Codrington Howard (9) — 121
Stephana Sojan (9) — 122
Jannat Azam (9) — 123
Oliver Cupi (9) — 124
Huda Boucetta (10) — 125
Angela Soares Da Costa (10) — 126
Liana Roopesh (10) — 127
Adina Nadeem-Aftab (10) — 128
Gafar El-Hassan (10) — 129
Kareem Osman (10) — 130
Riannah Bonifuse (10) — 131

Cora Destany Buron-Jackson (10)	132
Aimee Gardner Nott (9)	133
Sofia Sarwar (10)	134
Jette Wuerker (10)	135
Ayman Saadi Mahir (9)	136
Hadia Haydari (9)	137
Daniella Drizi (9)	138
Johana Jerish (10)	139
Nadine Da Silva (9)	140
Aadam Waqar (10)	141
Ritish Balu (9)	142
Yarai Georgeson-Campo (9)	143
Inaaya Bibi Asghar (10)	144
Konnor Jordan-Madden (9)	145

Woodlands CE Primary School, Woodlands

Olivia Moore (9)	146
Lily Newton (10)	147
Molly Holroyd (10)	148
Caylum Joseph Liu (10)	150
Thea Stilgoe (10)	151
Finlay Tempest (10)	152
Lilly Briscoe (9)	153
Millie Wood (10)	154
Jack Oliver Kay (9)	155
Dexter George Fish (10)	156
Ryleigh Wilkins (9)	157

THE POEMS

Smaker, He Is Not An Attacker!

Smaker the big monster is very funny,
He likes to eat jam and honey,
People look at him and run like a cheetah,
He has a sister whose name is Aneeta.
He is as fat as a pig,
He loves to get messy and dig.
He likes to play with little kids,
Smaker eats pens and lids.
He sleeps in trash
And for breakfast, he eats mash.
He has a drum that goes *bang!*
He stepped on the phone when it rang.
He breaks glasses and makes them smash,
He has never had a rash.
Smaker loves to eat jelly,
You will laugh if you see his huge belly.
If you see Smaker, welcome him in,
Make sure you don't poke him with a pin!

Amina Torofdar (10)
Andalusia Academy, St Matthias Park

The Monster That Lives Across Our Street

I have a new neighbour called Nelly,
Who is very strange, you see,
She has four hands and feet
And five eyes that stare at me!

Her skin is slimy and is as red as a cherry
And when she walks, she wobbles like jelly,
She slurps and burps as she gobbles up her nosh,
But don't be fooled, she is never crude,
In fact, she is very posh!

She has once met the Queen
And you will never find her being mean,
In fact, I am sure you would love to meet
My new neighbour monster that lives across our street!

Aisha Nounu (8)
Andalusia Academy, St Matthias Park

Spooky Loves To Scare!

Spooky loves to scare,
Only when he sees a bear.
He loves to dance,
He might put you in a trance.
Spooky runs around,
Only when he hears a loud sound.
Spooky loves his bed,
Don't turn him the colour red!
Spooky has jet-black hair,
His friends have a secret lair.
Spooky loves to play around,
If he doesn't, he will frown.
Spooky thinks he is scary,
Spooky's secret is he wants to see a fairy.
He also has a terrible smell,
He lives under a big shell.

Sumaya Saeed Awil (10)
Andalusia Academy, St Matthias Park

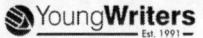

Transparent Minotaur

If you're walking through a maze
And you find yourself looking at arrows,
Don't turn left, if you do,
You will find lots of dangers ahead!
If you do survive through it,
You will find the most horrible creature on Earth;
A transparent Minotaur.
It has sharp horns and a thick tail,
A gigantic tummy to eat lots of things.
If you get personal with him,
You will have to run!
His footsteps stomp after me
As I fly through the maze...

Saifullah Ahmed Safdar (10)
Andalusia Academy, St Matthias Park

Buffly

Buffly the monster loves to jump around,
Sometimes her twin (doppelgänger), Muffly, stays on the ground.
She loves things that go up and down,
Bounce goes the sound when she jumps around.
Take her in and she will go *bing!*
She's fluffier than a teddy bear,
If you say that, she'll lock you in her lair!
Bing! Boing!
She'll make that sound when she's angry.

Aisha Sumaya Ahmed (10)
Andalusia Academy, St Matthias Park

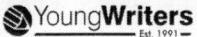

Slimy Sling

He slithers from under the bed,
His top eyes peek to see if you're fast asleep.
He wriggles out and messes up your toys,
He goes downstairs to eat your packed lunch.
He opens your juice with his fangs that are as sharp as a lion's teeth,
He goes and sucks up your packed lunch until it's gone,
I know all that because I am the monster...
And I ate your packed lunch!

Mumtaz Yoonis (9)
Andalusia Academy, St Matthias Park

Polo, The Scary Hairy Monster

Polo the scary, hairy, terrifying monster
Always running into trouble
Polo runs to the clumsy monsters
Polo can dash to get some cash
Polo can run into school and make trouble
Bang! Crash! Rumble!
Polo is hungry, he won't stop until he gets food
He lives in the trash after having a crash
Polo is the scariest, hairiest monster in town!

Azhaan Nadeem (9)
Andalusia Academy, St Matthias Park

Raven

Raven is scary
And hairy
He is like a snake
And he's late for school!

He thinks he's cool
But he's a fool
His breath smells like trash
And he makes people dash!

Raven roars like a lion!
And he has a friend called Brian
And he eats anything you give him.

Arhum Haroon (10)
Andalusia Academy, St Matthias Park

Ripcon

Ripcon is an unfriendly giant
He is as wild and hairy as the Hulk
He has a skeleton tattoo and a terrible smell
His rocket launcher can break things into chunks
He is as golden as the bright sun
He has a punk haircut.

Reye Mohamed Saad (10)
Andalusia Academy, St Matthias Park

Fabulous Fluffy

As bright as a light
As brave as a knight
Being short in height
But strong in a fight.

Saarah Hamid (8)
Andalusia Academy, St Matthias Park

Midnight And Scary Sky!

Scary Sky is a monster,
What kind of monster? you ask,
Well, I'll tell very, very soon,
Sky is as fluffy as a cloud,
As scary as a lion,
His long sharp teeth are as lethal as a sword,
Sky is as cute as a button,
But when the sun comes down,
His dark side corrupts him,
Sky's eyes start to roll,
His antennae start to twitch
And his eyes go fiery red,
He starts looking for his midnight snack,
What is his midnight snack? you ask,
Well think of Sky as a superhero,
He eats bad monsters,
So if you hear a sksksksk... you are safe,
Safe from bad...

Elyssa Stoker (10)
Argyle House School, Tunstall Road

Gnasher The Gruesome

Gnasher the Gruesome
Is a green, slimy chap
With eyes as red as blood
And claws that go *snap!*
He hides under the bed
Waiting for children to sleep
Then out he comes for a sneaky little peek.

With teeth as sharp as razors
He's quick on his feet
If the children spot him
He leaves them shaking like a leaf.

Beware of Gnasher the Gruesome
And check under your bed
Because if you miss him
He'll eat you like bread.

Lily Grace Mileham (7)
Argyle House School, Tunstall Road

Death Devil

I am Death Devil, the evilest monster you have ever seen!
Do not come to meet me unless you are very keen!
I don't play with children and toys!
I eat humans and little boys!
I am nocturnal and only come out at night!
Stay indoors my friends or be prepared for a fight!
Only the bravest of humans would come to see me!
Be warned as I will eat you for my tea!
In one gulp you'll be gone!
No longer here!
Come on now and try if you have no fear!

Joseph Allan Wheatley (8)
Argyle House School, Tunstall Road

The Unicorn Monster

You may think unicorns are light
But this one will give you a fright.
She's under your bed.
She's here for your head.
Rainbow has red eyes
And loves to tell lies.
Rainbow happily eats meat
And is breathing on my feet.
She has a friend called Max
Who never pays his tax.
Rainbow always leaves tracks
When she's eating her snacks.
I follow her down the stairs
But she never really cares!

Aneesha Kaur (9)
Argyle House School, Tunstall Road

Grumpy Fred And Me

Grumpy Fred is red
He feels dead
Because he just got out of bed
In the shed
And fell on his head!

Grumpy Fred gets in my head
Makes me mad and makes me sad
Sometimes he makes me laugh out loud
Because his grumps go round and round
His endless grumps go on and on
That's when I tell him to be gone

I will never be like Fred
I want to be happy in my head.

Molly Lancaster (7)
Argyle House School, Tunstall Road

Crystal's Story

My monster is silly and very wild,
She's really loud and not very mild.
She loves to have fun and play in the sea.
She loves to splash especially me.
She makes waves like a shark.
When she's scared in the dark
She hides under my bed.
When she has a bad head
She's not very scary
And that's fine with me.
That's the type of monster she will always be.

Holly Quinn (8)
Argyle House School, Tunstall Road

Pip, The Friendly, Helpful Alien

Pip, the friendly, helpful alien
Lives in my egg chair,
Every morning and night
He helps me brush my hair.

Pip, the friendly, helpful alien
Loves to eat my dinner,
Then he helps me on sports day
And makes me into a winner.

Pip, the friendly, helpful alien
Is my best friend,
We laugh and play together,
I will take care of him till the end.

Ellie Calvert (9)
Argyle House School, Tunstall Road

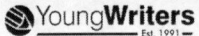

The Village Monster

Montia the monster, the village monster would appear at night.
She would mumble and grumble all through the night.
She would make the villagers very uptight.
They would hide with fear!
Because they didn't want her near
But all Montia wanted was a friendship to make her cheer!
They could play all day in the village or the town
Having fun and laughter and never a frown.

Grace Urwin (8)
Argyle House School, Tunstall Road

Giant Fluffy Horns

With hair as orange as a cheetah,
My monster growls and roars.
With a coat as fluffy as a sheep,
He crawls like a turtle.
Eyes like a laser,
My monster hypnotises people.
A wide purple mouth and a blueberry face,
My monster rumbles like the sea.
He has a slimy body that squelches like the mud.
I love my monster and he loves me.

Yara Abouleid (8)
Argyle House School, Tunstall Road

Slagling

Ten fingers, good for saying hi,
Nine horns, good for looks,
Eight toes, for wiggling about,
Seven ribs, nice and strong,
Six nostrils, for smelling dinner,
Five mouths, for chewing on his cereal,
Four limbs, a helping hand,
Three eyes, for finding his books,
Two hands, for hugging his friends,
One heart, to love everyone.

Aryan Batth (9)
Argyle House School, Tunstall Road

The Unhappy Vampire

I hate being like this,
Not going in the sunlight.
I can see it, why is it so pretty?
I hate only going outside at night
And the taste of blood
But I need it to survive.
Wandering at night is not so pleasant,
Stepping in dog poo is the worst part.
I wish I was a human again,
It would be the best.

Ajumoke Amy-Jean Maughan (8)
Argyle House School, Tunstall Road

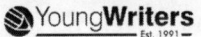

Mr Monster Munch

Stomp, stomp, stomp,
Monster Munch is looking for something to chomp.
Up the road, he sees a big shiny car
But he would much rather have a giant chocolate bar.
He comes out at night to find something to bite,
So children beware or you might get a scare!

Elliot Fallows George Paxton (9)
Argyle House School, Tunstall Road

Nightmare Fredbear

Nightmare Fredbear is a mean guy
Who walks at night stealing food.
In the morning he goes to bed
And sleeps all day.
He sometimes snores a scary snore.
He sometimes growls and bumps.
But Nightmare Fredbear is known for his fearsome scary jump scares.

Oliver Hunter (9)
Argyle House School, Tunstall Road

The Creeper

He moves without feet
Sliding through the air
Waiting for his next prey
To catch with his hair
Slowly, silently, he creeps
Without letting you out of his sight
Two yellow eyes as big as pies
Shining like the moon, so round and bright.

Brooke Frances Hunter (7)
Argyle House School, Tunstall Road

Frank The Footballing Monster

F rank is good at football.
R unning fast to score the goals
A nd never misses a thing because he has three eyes.
N ever a monster better than Frank at football.
K icks the ball, he never misses a shot.

Henry Hutchinson-Khan (8)
Argyle House School, Tunstall Road

Mr Slimy Fireball's Adventure

Mr Slimy Fireball was teleported from a different dimension.
He used to be naughty all the time
Which is why he got loads of detention.
He met a boy
Who turned Mr Slimy Fireball good.
His name was Troy.

Nathan Smith (11)
Argyle House School, Tunstall Road

Cutey And His Pugs

My name is Cutey Monster
And I love giving hugs
I love going on walks every day with my little pugs
Every morning, I wake up with my pugs
In my bed as snug as a rug.

Summer Lily Marshall-Graham (7)
Argyle House School, Tunstall Road

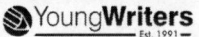

The Cookie Monster

The Cookie Monster craved cream cookies.
The Cookie Monster was not nice.
One time, he ate cookies twice!
The Cookie Monster gives everybody a fright in the night.

Jasmin Kaur (7)
Argyle House School, Tunstall Road

Snowy Monster

Snowy, Snowy,
Please come quick.
It is snowing very, very thick.
If you don't come quick,
You will melt so very quick!

Oscar Smiles (8)
Argyle House School, Tunstall Road

The Three-Tailed Fox

Sneaky Sam is a three-tailed fox.
He is so very sneaky, as sneaky as a mouse!
And as fast as a cheetah stalking its prey.

He likes to chase birds and eat them for his dinner
He pins a bird to the ground and there it lies.

Sneaky Sam is a terribly clever fox, cleverer than any other fox
Because he is a three-tailed fox
A very rare fox, which makes him the leader of the foxes...

All because of his three tails.

Bronwyn Holden (8)
Birdham CE Primary School, Birdham

The Monster Poem

M ind so big with pieces that are like chips inside
O n his nose, he has a spot that is like a little mountain
N ot his legs, he slithers along like a snake going slow
S cary as a wolf with sharp teeth that will rip you apart
T he creaking sound of his electric head as he turns around
E yes flash in your mind
R ed spikes as sharp as knives.

Fraizer Golds (8)
Birdham CE Primary School, Birdham

Monster

M y monster has fourteen poisonous spikes
O n the top of the mountain, there lives a monster and he sleeps on ice-cold snow
N asty as a saltwater crocodile
S pikes down his back and tail
T errifying claws as he gets them cut
E ating fast as he runs through the terrifying forest
R ough on his tail as you stroke him.

Amy Leigh Tebbs (8)
Birdham CE Primary School, Birdham

Furry Fang

M arvellously magical and monstrous
O range teeth and colourful body
N aughty as a monkey scoffing food
S cary like a shark eating people up in one gulp
T errible and terrific, Furry Fang is very friendly
E verywhere he goes, he leaves a trail of slime
R oaring as loud as a lion, Furry Fang never eats people.

Niamh Munnery (8)
Birdham CE Primary School, Birdham

Very Cute

M ean glare
O blivious
N oisy
S lits for eyes
T empered
E ating mad machine
R ight? No, not right

Not mean, no slits, cute
As humongous as an elephant, but...
As fluffy as a budgie with extra feathers
As cute as a newborn baby chick
And always in need of a cuddle.

Lillie Lowery (9)
Birdham CE Primary School, Birdham

Monster

M y medium monster wears medium clothes
O ut of the human world, there is a stylish city called Monster City
N ow Monster City is in a beautiful town
S tyle is all they care about
T -shirts, dresses and more
E very day, a different outfit is seen
R ough coats everywhere.

Ava Richards (8)
Birdham CE Primary School, Birdham

Mouldy Monsters

M arvellous monsters make biscuits
O range caves are pitch-black
N oisy fun is for everyone
S awing fangs tear up buildings
T hey are as scary as jaw-dropping tarantulas
E lastic bands get shot everywhere when humans are in Monster Town
R ipping through giant rocks.

Florence Wilson (8)
Birdham CE Primary School, Birdham

Monster Diary

M onster sees through the human flesh
O n the beach, the water monsters lie
N o monsters go near the city
S ea is not a place to go, monsters stay in the deep
T obad, the flesh-ripper
E ating time, they munch on children
R oo is one of Bing-Bong's friends.

George Sheperd (8)
Birdham CE Primary School, Birdham

My Monster

M y monster is spiky and small
O range and green antennae on his head
N oisy, slippery and blue all over
S pots as yellow as the African desert
T eeth as sharp as prickly thorns
E yes as round as dinner plates
R oars like a lion waiting to catch its prey.

Darcey Louise Nunn Knowles (9)
Birdham CE Primary School, Birdham

Monster

M ighty monsters wreck the Earth
O h my gosh, there's a monster killing the Earth
N o, my spikes are getting more and more broken by the second
S o many monsters
T urning into destruction mode
E ven a tremor is coming
R ed spikes all over his face!

Marcus Irvine-Smith (8)
Birdham CE Primary School, Birdham

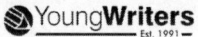

Monster Penguin

M onsters can be scary
O r they can be cute
N one are quite as freaky as the one I saw
S harp teeth lay in its mouth
T hat thing just can't be beaten
E ven his eyes make you want to kiss him but
R ed blood drips down to his feet.

Joshua Ellis (8)
Birdham CE Primary School, Birdham

The Monster Fish

M onster swimming in the ocean
O gling at the view
N asty needles piercing people
S lithering and slimy like a slimy snake
T wisting and turning, trembling tides
E scape from the monster fish!
R ough running people, away, get away!

Fallon Cole (8)
Birdham CE Primary School, Birdham

Monster

M agnificent, marvellous monsters
O ogling monsters creeping into your room
N ot cute at all
S erious fangs in his mouth
T he gun-shooting nails
E ats everything that comes near to him
R eptile that could eat everything.

Bertie Jones (8)
Birdham CE Primary School, Birdham

Monster

M *unch, munch, munch*
O xygen-making monster
N ever stand too close
S canning through the trees like a hunter in the woods
T eeth like thorns
E ats anything that comes near
R ests only when it's raining.

Max Sargent (9)
Birdham CE Primary School, Birdham

Monster

M ysterious, marvellous, master shape-shifter
O utside, waiting for sunrise
N ever to get phased... not today
S o get some chicken otherwise you're dinner
T eatime!
E very day, a chicken dies
R *oar!*

Dexter Drew (8)
Birdham CE Primary School, Birdham

Monster Mayhem

He is furry like my teddy bear lying on my bed
He roars like a rocket taking off in the middle of the night
He has four dangly, long arms so don't venture near
Look, his spiky horns are like 5,000 needles on your back
So beware, approach him at your peril.

Ernie Livings (10)
Birdham CE Primary School, Birdham

Monster

M onsters as spiky as a pineapple
O gling on the water
N ever-ending squishy bones
S aw it had super sharp teeth
T hat thing is impossible to beat
E ven its eyes are red and black
R oars like a dinosaur.

Beau Madden (8)
Birdham CE Primary School, Birdham

Monster Of The Water

M agnificent, mischievous beast
O perating the grill to move along
N oisy like a buzzing saw
S eaweed makes him invisible
T echnology makes him wake
E yes see everything
R ed, shimmering scales.

Thomas Bacon (9)
Birdham CE Primary School, Birdham

Monster

M y monster has fifteen legs
O n his head, he has long antennae
N its in his hair
S pikes down his back
T ints in his skin
E ggs through their hair
R ough, scaly wings flapping through the air.

Raf Kennedy (8)
Birdham CE Primary School, Birdham

Daniel, The Half Spaniel

Teeth like daggers or jagged shark's teeth
As cute as a penguin when it's diving in an icy sea
Furry like a rabbit or a golden spaniel's belly
Eyes as black as coal or the hole in space
Beware, don't touch, but he is cute!

Fynn Cornwell (8)
Birdham CE Primary School, Birdham

Jeffery Who's Very, Very Pesky

He's as hungry as a lion on a steel chain
Who's been sitting there for nearly a day!

He gives a wary, menacing look
Just like a dragon took

And he made such a roar,
Just like you would hear if you met a boar.

Charlie Graham Ashdown (8)
Birdham CE Primary School, Birdham

Jellypus' Life

Jellypus is cruel, very cruel indeed
But only to little fish, not like you or I
He has an infinite lifespan, unless murdered
But nobody can survive the pressure
With a happy time
No fish is brave enough to go too near.

Edward Palmer-Felgate (8)
Birdham CE Primary School, Birdham

Blobo

B ig, green, calm and beautiful
L ook out! He's not what he seems
O bviously he becomes angry when...
B lack and red wings appear
O ffensive to everyone.

Zia Mahmood-Jones (8)
Birdham CE Primary School, Birdham

Shake Those Rusty Bones

Shake those rusty bones
And shivers in your spine
Make those bones mine
By the time you get them back
I will stab you in the back
If you are still alive
We will eat you alive.

Joe Tranchant (8)
Birdham CE Primary School, Birdham

Jeff The Monster

J eff is the naughtiest monster ever.
E very night he sneaks out of my bed to go and eat all of the children.
F or bed Jeff wears his blue and white stripy pyjamas.
F or bed he also wears his blue slippers.

T he children are always asleep when Jeff eats them.
H e always takes my sweets.
E verybody is scared of him.

M y monster always cuddles me when I'm cold.
O ver the hills he runs when I'm asleep to find more children to eat.
N obody likes Jeff, everyone's scared.
S weets are one of his favourite things.
T he children are terrified of him.
E verybody hates him, everybody stays away.
"R un children, watch out, he's coming to eat you!"

Kayla-May Palmer (9)
Hillside Academy, Denaby Main

The Monster Under My Bed

I heard a noise under my bed
It was sighing and sighing
I put my head under the bed
I saw a cute, cuddly monster
It was hugging my teddy bear
With care on the chair
I gave him a pear on the chair.

He had lots of hair.
When he was on the chair
He brushed his hair
And brushed the monster.
His name is Jubbly
Really cute and soft.

Alicia Murray (10)
Hillside Academy, Denaby Main

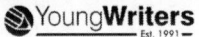

Scary Monster

I can hear a scary monster
It's coming to eat my tummy tum tum
So I'm going to run, run, run
Monsters like treats so is she going to eat?
Don't stop, shout, shout, shout
I need a break to wakey wake
So I sit on a chair to brush my hair
Then I run to get a can
So then I run to go back.

Jessica Lockett (9)
Hillside Academy, Denaby Main

The Square Head Monster

M ik the monster
O n the ground in the mud
N ext to his bed are mud pies
S mall body so he can hide
T eeth like a bear
E yes so big so he can see really well
R eally big ears to listen for children.

Millie Cooper (9)
Hillside Academy, Denaby Main

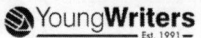

Bob From Downstairs

When I go to bed
It always eats my bread
I go downstairs to look at my wall
Then I look down the hall.

I go back to bed to sleep
I hear creaks from the bad monster
But it is just Bob the Freezer!

Cody Dodd (9)
Hillside Academy, Denaby Main

My Monster

This morning I found a monster
He looked like a fluffy pheasant
He looked cute
I asked for his name
He said Bloop
He is kind
He is so spotty
He is totally not scary
He has a giant tummy.

Denver Leigh Mathieson (9)
Hillside Academy, Denaby Main

There's A Monster Under Your Bed!

There was a boy called Ted
He thought there was a monster under his bed
It glided like a plane, slid like a snake
Every night, Ted said,
"Mum! I think there's a monster under my bed!"
Then Mum replied saying, "Now you're just being silly, Ted!"
Then Ted protests, "But Mum, it's true!
It's going to jump out at you!"
Scatter! Scatter! Scatter!
"What was that? said Ted, shivering
"Oh, maybe it was just the cat," said Mum, trembling
Then they stopped, they looked behind them
Roar!
There was a monster!
He screamed in fright, "I am a night fright!"

Jasiah McDermott (8)
Jessop Primary School, Herne Hill

My Monster

My monster wakes up at night
He sneaks into children's bedrooms
And he takes and eats their brains
He smashes through windows and doors
He smashes through stones in all the children's gardens
Children, look out!

Francisco Jackson (5)
Jessop Primary School, Herne Hill

Greedy Monsters

Greedy monsters like Greedy Gobbler are never in a very good mood
They always grumble and grunt
Greedy Gobbler loves food
You could see him sneaking from the cupboard in house four
He lives under the bed and nothing more
He comes out in the dead of night
Waiting to frighten little children
If children are naughty
He always has something to say
His fur is also dark blue
At the end of his tail is an enormous club that he thumps on the ground all night
He is a rude monster that burps an awful lot
He slithers across streets and rooms, trying not to be seen
He loves an old building with damp rooms
His horns are as sharp as knives and his teeth are rancid
Blood curls out of his mouth and his legs are short and thin

His nose is pointy, his tongue sticks out all the time
and his horns are yellow
He has antennae with eyes and mouths at the end
He has wings as blue as Pluto.

Caroline Morgans (7)
St Christophers Academy, Dunstable

The Dark!

The night is where the monsters come out
The night is where the monsters come for you
The night is where the ghosts come out
The night is where the monsters sleep
The night is where the monsters run around
The night is where the monsters chase kids
The night is where the monsters go
The night is where the monsters get food
The night is where the monsters go for Halloween
The night is where the monsters clip their toenails
The night is where the monsters cut their hair
The night is where the monsters scare the kids
The night is where the monsters go to the shops
The night is where the monsters go and read books
The night is where the monsters go to KFC
The night is where the monsters go to Donald Trump
The night is where the monsters go to McDonald's
The night is where the monsters go to the playground.

Macey Joseph (7)
St Christophers Academy, Dunstable

My Bloodthirsty Bow

B ig Bloodthirsty Bow is enormous
L uck of not getting haunted in your dreams, probably zero
O verall, he is scary but really, he's friendly
O ne eye he has, beady and crimson, plus another eleven on his head
D o you know his tongue will flicker tentatively?
T he friendly beast is really rancid, really how long has he been without a shower?
H is tongue as long as a metre
I would completely call him a disgrace
R eally never ever meet him
S pikes as sharp as thorns
T oo many eyes on his head really
Y ou should be terrified

B lankets over your head but you're not safe
O n every point, there are spikes
W ings creepier than sharks.

Zaynab Sheikh (7)
St Christophers Academy, Dunstable

The Terrifying Monster

Painting is what my monster loves
Well, his gloves don't fit
What he dreams of is a friendly monster
But what could happen is a bad monster in the street
With the burning heat
An actual evil monster
He is anxious of what might happen
He might come in the house with his bad claws
And look through the drawers
Roar around, looking for prey
"What? A dog?" he said
There was a dog sitting on a log outside the window
He goes to school the next day and on the way
He sees some hay and picks some up
But the monster comes and his name is Paint Your Mother Green
The child monster gets scared, his eyes are glistening
He does love children but not in a good way

He says lies but he has stupid eyes
He is a scary monster but his friends say, "I don't care!"

Oliver Woodall (7)
St Christophers Academy, Dunstable

Doofy's Adventure

Monster Doofy is a bit like Goofy,
He was clapping along, singing a song in a very joyful way
What he had done (he named Pung) was bang rocks on his head.
He found a child wearing black,
wearing a bag on her back
Doofy said, "Hi Miss Wigglebottom, are you wearing only cotton?"
Miss Wigglebottom shouted, "No! Do you want to get some Jell-O?"
Doofy said, "No. I'm going to bang you on my head."
So he did, *bang boo! Wupty woo!*
Doofy went on a rocket with nothing in his pocket.
He went to space with a good suitcase
that he got from Miss Wigglebottom
He arrived on the moon and found a balloon flying in the sky
His mum came and said,
"You need to go to bed!"

Theo Kiely (8)
St Christophers Academy, Dunstable

Dummy Gummy Slug

This monster is a snuggly monster
This monster is a brave monster
This monster is an evil, sharp, square-eyed monster
This monster is a straight moustached monster
This monster is a charming, fierce monster
This monster is a tight, rounded monster
This monster is an icy, delicate monster
This monster is a drawing slug monster
This monster is a rude monster
This monster is a beaming, nibbly, tasty monster
This monster is a dazzling drop monster
This monster is a puzzling monster
This monster is a poorly monster
This monster is a youngster monster
This monster is a yawning monster
This monster is a solving monster
This monster is a clashing monster.

Tom McCarthy (7)
St Christophers Academy, Dunstable

The Human Body Blob

Hello! I'm a smart-looking, friendly monster
I might have an egg-shaped head
So if you want to be my friend, be extra careful
Touch or scratch my head
And a liquid that smells like rotten eggs
Comes out, so watch out!
I never change my pants
They are as tight as two walls pushing you
I keep my clothes clean and tidy and neat
My red and white tie is 100,000,000,
256,708,946,720,236cm long
So I have to fold it 2,000 times
It takes about five years to fold it!
I have a pet bag that is alive
I eat barbecues and when I go to a restaurant, I eat it rare
I am 567,821,008,756,210,000,089,216,502 years old!

Jacob Jojo (7)
St Christophers Academy, Dunstable

A Hidden Monster

A hidden monster is somewhere in a dull house
A hidden monster can smell a sparkling mouse

A hidden monster is somewhere in a room
A hidden monster doesn't have a bendy broom

A hidden monster made an extremely loud bang
A hidden monster, the bells have rung

A hidden monster did not do a slurp
A hidden monster did a gigantic burp

A hidden monster is all red
A hidden monster can go in a shed

A hidden monster broke a chair
A hidden monster cannot fly in the air

A hidden monster, that was what he'd done
A hidden monster will spook everyone.

Bright Onunwa (7)
St Christophers Academy, Dunstable

Creepy Bubbler

C ross when he loses battles
R ough when he gets tough
E ggs that he throws
E ats greedily
P oops on his bubbles
Y awns when he burps

M ysterious roars
O pens doors easily
N ags when he's angry
S obs when he's sad
T astes human blood
E xpert at fighting
R ings people's doorbells as loud as he can
S cares people away.

I'm coming to get you!

Inaaya Ahmed (7)
St Christophers Academy, Dunstable

Shape-Shifter

S caly as a snake
H e is very hairy as he does not brush his fur
A t the end of his dreams, he wants to be a star
P lanet Mars is his favourite planet
E normous as an elephant, tall like a giant
-
S pots as big as a mountain
H elpful as us
I ncredible as you
F urry as a dog
T errifying as a devil
E normous feet that make a hole in the ground
R ancid breath as he doesn't brush.

Pallavi Pandya (7)
St Christophers Academy, Dunstable

Spotty Pop Monster

This monster is intelligent
This monster is hungry
This monster is thirsty
This monster lives in Bob Town made out of men
This monster is the leader of Bob Town
This monster is spotty
This monster is a bad boy
This monster has a rancid tummy
His friend is Ald-C-Sam
Do whatever he says
His little brother stinks of rancid bins
His rancid tongue is stinky
His breath is stinky too
His spotty dots are so scary
And as fluffy as a cuddly bear.

Felix Owen Davies (8)
St Christophers Academy, Dunstable

Terrifying Lion

His claws are as sharp as spikes
He will kick you out and roar in your face
He lies to children and eats them for dinner
He likes slime and he will dump it on your head
He will prank you by turning invisible
He lives in a cave and only comes out at night
He only sleeps in the day
He will sleep in rocks and be happy but grumpy
He will never smile when he eats
Or does something fun
He will prick you with his spikes
Also, be cold for Christmas.

Jessica Bell-Cooper (7)
St Christophers Academy, Dunstable

What Is Slimer?

My monster lives on Earth
He likes to creep out children
He does not wash himself
He does not wash his teeth
He is so stinky, no monster goes near him
He does not care anyway

He is so slimy and disgusting
He does not sing, he hates it
He likes to eat
He is as smelly as an armpit
He likes to break things
He hates reading
He likes to sleep

And most of all, he likes to creep out every child in the world.

Franek Kloza (7)
St Christophers Academy, Dunstable

Roar, Roar, Roar

This monster can eat its toes
This monster can grumble all day
This monster can sting the children
This monster can fly in the sky

This monster can sprint around
This monster can kill a vampire
This monster can jump on a roof
This monster can roar, roar, roar

This monster can scratch a wall
This monster can scream along
This monster can heal with a lick
This monster can go to sleep.

Jasmine Dhesi (7)
St Christophers Academy, Dunstable

Mean Little Monster

"**M** ean little monster," says Mum
"**O** h dear, don't get filthy in a puddle of mud!
  N o, don't go, finish your food young lady.
  S melly, pungent breath indeed, no surprise for you
  T ell yourself to get out of bed
  E arn that gold medal!" she said
"**R** ampage little monster, don't chop off the flower's head!"

Samantha Nnadozie (7)
St Christophers Academy, Dunstable

Little Fluffy Horns

F urry as a pillow
L ong as a ruler
U nited with his friends
F luffy is a round ball
F rightened like a spider
Y oung as a newborn chick

H elpful like a firefighter
O ur monster friend is patient
R espectful as a teacher
N ever ever ever gives up
S oon goes to bed to get a good night's sleep.

Grace Daniels (7)
St Christophers Academy, Dunstable

Fluffy Rainbow Sparkle Doodle's Candy Land

Candy Land is where monsters live
Candy Land is sweet and tasty
Candy Land is where only good monsters live
Candy Land has rainbows and unicorns
Candy Land is where my monster lives
Candy Land is cute and girly
Candy Land is lovely and glamourous
Candy Land is where children play with their monsters
Candy Land is an astonishing place
If you visit, you will want to stay.

Ellie Cook (7)
St Christophers Academy, Dunstable

Slimer

S ticks to anything he wants to
L ikes bananas and hoops that twinkle astonishingly
I t is a shape-shifter monkey that hates butts
M arvellous sharp teeth that rip metal to its death
E ating trash at night and maybe you, he has a hammer at the end of his tail
R eally, he is a helpful monster who likes benevolent humans.

Farhaan Ali Sarwar (7)
St Christophers Academy, Dunstable

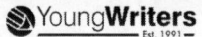

Strider Licker's Adventure

S trolling on an adventure
T icking on the clock
R ip up the tops
I n the rocks
D eck the knocks
E nd the dogs
R um is a log

L ick the fog
I n the house
C ome the wheels
K ick the cats
E at the adults
R ats to eat.

William Kimberley (7)
St Christophers Academy, Dunstable

Monsters Poem

Monsters are black
Monsters are green
Monsters are different
Just like me

Monsters can be scary
Monsters can be funny
Monsters can be disgusting
When their noses are runny

Monsters come during the day
Monsters come during the night
Monsters come whenever
Just to give you a fright.

Mia Rose (7)
St Christophers Academy, Dunstable

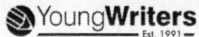

The Dark Monster

A terrifying monster with really rancid breath
A terrifying monster who has razor-sharp claws
A terrifying monster who has wrinkly eyes that are rude
A terrifying monster who has terrifying teeth
That are as sharp as 1,000,000 snakes
A terrifying monster who scares you half to death.

George Kimberley (7)
St Christophers Academy, Dunstable

Hungry Terrifying Tim

Hungry Terrifying Tim
Decided to go for a swim
He swam under the water
And bumped into danger
And tricked her then bit her
Hungry Terrifying Tim defeated.

Surayya Dauhoo (8)
St Christophers Academy, Dunstable

Friendly Fred

Friendly Fred is a charming monster
He likes to bring joy to children
He delivers dazzling presents
And helps them up when they fall over.

Riley Battams (7)
St Christophers Academy, Dunstable

The Monster Humans Have Created

He is terrifying and as tall as a house,
He makes me feel as small as a mouse.
As he runs towards me, the ground cracks,
Plastic bottles are tangled in the hair on his back.
He has yellow claws,
Or are they plastic drinking straws?
This monster is angry, ugly and hairy,
He reminds me that the future of our planet is scary!

Oozing green slime and covered in dead fish and fleas,
He has come from the polluted water of our seas.
He has tin cans for teeth and bright orange eyes,
"Put your waste in the right bins!" he cries.
I feel his anger and his pain,
It's time to stop deforestation and acid rain.
This monster is terrifying and is coming for you,
It's time to recycle, reuse and renew!

Ava Jessica Peppiatt (10)
St Peter's CE Middle School, Old Windsor

Zorg The Trickster

There once was a monster called Zorg,
Who was always really bored

He liked to be naughty, playing bits of tricks,
And thought his moves were always sick!

He would jump up high and throw eggs on your head,
And when you were sleeping, he'd put worms in your bed

When you wake up, there would be beans in your shoes
If you went to the bathroom, you would find toilet roll wrapped around the loo

Beware of the food fight at lunchtime to begin
Have your sandwiches, yoghurts and crisps ready, but you won't win!

After a long day of being naughty,
He dreams of what to do
But be careful of Zorg,
He could play his next trick on you.

Rocco Valentine Eastell (10)
St Peter's CE Middle School, Old Windsor

Fiery

There was once a strange, funny creature,
Who had ever so funny features
He had big, bulging eyes,
He wore a striped tie
He was a ball of fluff, orange and red,
He liked to sleep under my bed!
He had those very long legs,
That were held together by some pegs
His nose was big, squashy and round,
He had a power that made him disappear into the ground
My furry friend was so naughty but nice,
The strangest thing, he said everything twice
He liked to protect me in the night,
Whoever came near, he gave a fright
He is so very special to me,
He loves to drink tea
He's my crazy monster, Fiery.

Maisy Eva Wood (10)
St Peter's CE Middle School, Old Windsor

Sheryl The Shape-Shifter!

This monster can shape-shift from animal to human to you!
Is there anything she can't do?
I highly doubt it!
She could be a proud peacock
Or an annoying nit
She shape-shifts through boredom
As there is nothing to do
She thinks, *let's make this life interesting,*
'Cause a palaver
Oh, she does love a bit of drama
She's my best friend
You ought to know
She's amazing at hide-and-seek
And though I pretend not to peek
I have to as I won't find her for a week
She's clever, cunning, courageous and more
Which is why she will be my best friend for sure.

Isabella Katherine Ann Spurling (10)
St Peter's CE Middle School, Old Windsor

The Honeybee Monster

Honey, Honeybee Monster
Walks on the land from the shore
He sleeps in the tree no more
He came a knocking on my door
I'd never seen this Honeybee Monster before
Honey, Honeybee Monster wanted to stay with me
because it was cold in the tree
Honey, Honeybee Monster had to sleep on the floor
Because he would snore and snore
Honey, Honeybee Monster had little pet bees
They made me sneeze and sneeze!
So the Honey, Honeybee Monster had to return to his tree
He couldn't stay with me
Honey, Honeybee Monster flew to a new Honey tree
But he stayed friends with me.

Honeysuckle Moon Morris (10)
St Peter's CE Middle School, Old Windsor

The Monster Scream

M assive, bulging eyes
O minous, low growl
N asty, horrendous teeth
S limy, slippery scales to slither
T errifying talons to rip its victims, limb by limb
E bony-black ears that prick up at the slightest sound
R otten toes embedded with fungus

S creeching like fingernails on a chalkboard
C ounting to ten, hoping it's a bad dream
R etreating under my blanket... petrified
E ngrossed in the horrific sounds surrounding me
A scream... a very loud scream
M aking me lose my final breath.

Sirut Kaur Hayre (10)
St Peter's CE Middle School, Old Windsor

The Sleep Monster's Secrets

Beware when you have shut your eyes,
Beware of slime on the floor
Beware of a three-eyed monster,
Who may just hear you snort
Beware of something you may think,
Was not there before
For this terrible beast can shape-shift,
And magically open the door
He roams through children's bedrooms,
Waiting for them to sleep
Trying to take them up,
You must not make a peep
One thing you can listen out for,
It is very easy to hear
He really can't breathe quietly,
So just open up your ears!
Beware of the sleep monster!

Josie Clarke (10)
St Peter's CE Middle School, Old Windsor

Autismo, The Mysterious Monster

My monster is autistic and as clever as can be
He has amazing hearing and eyesight you see
He sees the world differently from you and me
He has powers as strong as lightning
And that's what you can see
When he's angry, everything is a blur
To make himself feel better, he strokes his green fur
His head is all fuzzy,
He has four arms, two legs
And if you make him happy
He lays chocolate eggs!
He is a friendly monster
Has lots of friends too
He wants to help others
To make them laugh too.

Ella Louise Taylor (10)
St Peter's CE Middle School, Old Windsor

The Sabre-Toothed Huggle

On the way to school
I met a monster, all fluffy and blue
He wasn't a lost pet,
He was about six foot two
His teeth were pointy and white
Yet he was a fun, friendly creature
When he asked to go fly a kite
"Of course," said my teacher
We felt the wind pull the kite string
We smelt a barbecue in the distance
We played on the swings
And then climbed up the trees
Today was amazing
I hope Huggles is craving
Today was just brill
I hope Huggles visits again
He said he will!

Sohana Jhanji (10)
St Peter's CE Middle School, Old Windsor

Albert The Sleeping Monster

Albert the sleeping lump
He really isn't that plump
He has one fang
That would make a big bang
Whenever he began to snore
He can be such a bore
He sleeps all day and is awake all night
Albert hates the light

He is extremely short,
About the size of the loaf of bread you just bought

His wings are like a carpet beater
About half a metre
So if you see a monster at night,
Don't get a fright!
The little monster is likely to be Albert,
And he's alright.

Charlotte Stoner (10)
St Peter's CE Middle School, Old Windsor

The Monster That's Under My Bed

I hear him at night
I see him in the morning
He gives a warning,
Before frightening me in the morning!

He steals my things all the time,
Why, oh, why is he under my bed?
Help me get him out, if you dare

Help me, oh help me
I'm petrified!

I'm as pale as a ghost
I'm paranoid

I hear him at night
I see him in the morning
He gives me a warning
Before frightening me in the morning

Boom! Oh no! He's coming!

Sophie Harrap (10)
St Peter's CE Middle School, Old Windsor

The Monster In The Moon

Gooble has fangs, horns and short, spotty hair
And he loves to visit the fair
Gooble goes on rides that go up and down
And he screams as he goes around and around
When he eats ice cream, he fills up with air
And when he farts, he floats up in the air
Oh, how he loves to float above the fair
Watching people and lights from way up there
Waving and laughing from above the clouds
When night-time comes, he sits on the moon
And if you look closely, he's waving at you!

Cailley Bristow (10)
St Peter's CE Middle School, Old Windsor

A Day In The Life Of Coddie

Coddie is small, friendly and cute
On Jupiter, Starbursts are his favourite fruit
He has a friend, Neek,
He is as strong as can be
Every day after school, they would play hide-and-seek
In school, he is top of the class
His favourite subject is studying Mars
He flies to school because he is fast
Saying, "Good day," to every monster he passed
After tea every night,
Reading a book in bed with his mum
He finally falls asleep
After a day full of fun.

Annabel Crilly-McKean
St Peter's CE Middle School, Old Windsor

Xyrus The Titan

There was a titan called Xyrus
Who walked the Earth long ago
His records are written in papyrus
And he harnessed the power of snow

Knees quake whenever he's walking
Humans are his favourite meal
Trees shake whenever he's talking
And his heart is made out of steel

Whenever he threw a punch
You knew you were long gone
He'd probably eat you for lunch
Think you could slay him? You're most likely wrong.

Matthew Newell (11)
St Peter's CE Middle School, Old Windsor

Frightened Of Fang

I saw a monster under the bed
With beady eyes that were coloured red
He had teeth as sharp as razors
And three feet that couldn't step over lasers
I could smell the seeping slime coming out of his mouth
I think he's a monster from the south
He jumps out and scares you as he's so sly
He always finds a way to make me cry
"Fang, you mischievous monster, please go away
And leave me to sleep until the next day!"

Tilly Wright (10)
St Peter's CE Middle School, Old Windsor

Oddball

Oddball is huge,
Oddball is scary,
Oddball is fat,
Oddball is hairy!

Oddball doesn't cry,
Oddball doesn't laugh,
Oddball doesn't do much,
Apart from barf!

Oddball he eats,
Oddball he sleeps,
Oddball he jumps,
Oddball he leaps

This poem, in the end,
Probably won't become a trend,
But what matters,
Is that Oddball is my friend!

Phoebe Farmer (10)
St Peter's CE Middle School, Old Windsor

Claw Behind The Door

Beware, beware... under the stairs,
There lives a creature with curly black hair.
He's huge and slithery and sleeps all day,
But every night he comes out to play.
He likes to eat toes dangling out of bed,
But when you wake to look, he has always fled.
He hides under the bed or behind the door,
He's ugly, slimy, black and calls himself Claw.

Elliot Whitehorn (10)
St Peter's CE Middle School, Old Windsor

The Crimson Chaos Dragon

The Crimson Chaos Dragon is dark
He likes to lurk in the park
The deathly dragon hates being constructive
He leaps with glee when he is at his most destructive
The Crimson Chaos Dragon likes to lurk in the shadows
But he is always wary of flying arrows
When he flaps his wings, all the children shudder
Then they turn and run to their mothers.

Redmond Barron-Cheeseman (10)
St Peter's CE Middle School, Old Windsor

Monsters

M any different creatures walk around
O n a night like tonight
N ot because it's Christmas
S o let's all stop singing 'Jingle Bells'!
T his is because it's Halloween soon
E veryone beware
R eal monsters walk around
S aying, "Trick or treat!" everywhere.

Avarni Kaur Purewal (11)
St Peter's CE Middle School, Old Windsor

My Bubblegum Monster

I can hear a noise coming from the fridge
I can see the glitter leaking through the door

I can feel the pink eyes watching me,
But then... there is nothing there

Suddenly, there is a... *monster!*

I can see its cute face,
I can feel its pink fluff,
Then I say, "You are my bubblegum monster!"

Kayla Whitehead (10)
St Peter's CE Middle School, Old Windsor

Cleo

I'm as wide as I am tall,
And as round as a ball
My four googly eyes to terrify
Yellow in colour, hair on my back
Living all alone in my little shack!
I'm actually not scary,
But gentle like a canary!
Approach me and see,
I won't sting like a bee
I'm really quite funny,
And rather like honey.

May Hollick (10)
St Peter's CE Middle School, Old Windsor

Mimi The Monster

She is so cute
Especially when she plays the flute
Mimi is very fun
She likes to run
She is quite short
So she does not easily get caught
She is a little bit hairy
But not too scary
She can also fly
But she's all mine!

Leya Oulahsein (10)
St Peter's CE Middle School, Old Windsor

Scowl

Scowl is his name
Just like his face
Vicious and scary
Scaly and cunning
He lurks in the night
Gigantic as a mountain
Obnoxious as Wolverine
Ready to frighten and terrify!

Oskar Edward Thompson Totten (10)
St Peter's CE Middle School, Old Windsor

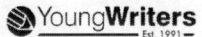

MasterChef/Monster Chef

Grizelda is my name,
You won't know from where I came,
Because you can be too scared,
But I'm not from under your bed.
I like baking cakes,
No matter how long it takes.
My favourite one
Is chocolate cake with jumpy bug jam.
I saw a poster on a tree
And I thought the MasterChef would be me!
I promise my cake will be delicious
And I'll take away your empty dishes.
I will add some special ingredients too
And it will blow off your shoe.
Okay, let's make it ready!
And the judges won't be greedy.
I will add some monster claws
And it will crack in your jaws.
It is time for the judges to make their decision,
But when they ate the monster cake
They started singing like singers in Eurovision.

I got first place!
For the amazing taste.
Now I will tell you where I'm from -
I'm from your oven door!

Klaudia Stawinska (9)
Wood Farm Primary School, Headington

Barr Barr's Adventure

One day Barr Barr went out
Because she heard a shout
But there was no one out,
She's sure she heard a shout no doubt,
She was sneaky,
So she had a sneak in a peek,
But still, nobody was about.
Because of this sneakiness
People say she's got some creepiness,
But I think she's just misunderstood.
Barr Barr is also shy
But she won't cry,
She is fine.
She is only shy because of her eye,
One is bigger than the other, that is why.
Barr Barr went further out,
But the more she did that, people would still scream and shout.
She had no clue why until she saw this pie,
Inside the pie was a note,
'There is no doubt you could figure this out,

You're a scary monster that just casually wanders about!'
Said the note and now Barr Barr decided to go figure herself out.

Kai Davies (10)
Wood Farm Primary School, Headington

Midnight Monster

I hear a noise in the corridor,
Or could it be my brother knocking on the door?
Suddenly the cuckoo clock chimes midnight,
Hopefully, that clock wasn't right,
Because when it's midnight bad things happen,
I'm not scared, what's the worse that can happen...?

I get out of bed and look into the garden,
Nothing's there that I'm not aware of,
I turn around for a second,
I look again and there it is,
A figure with horns,
Slimy green skin and claws...

I crawl into bed very scared,
I put my hand under the bed,
The same slimy green hand holds my hand,
I thought about any book with monsters in it,
Then an idea pops into my head,
I read a book about monsters last night,
Could it be the same monster clutching me tight...?

Merlin Monson (9)
Wood Farm Primary School, Headington

Ted

They say he likes to roam the streets
And little children are what he eats,
But this is not true, I've seen him before.
Listen to me, the story is not a bore.
I was passing a park, to get to the shops,
When I heard someone crying and sniffing lots.
I walked into a bush and saw a sight.
A fluffy blue monster crying, with his eyes shut tight.
"What's wrong?" I asked over all of his moans.
"Nothing," he said in a sad tone.
I remembered the bright yellow ball from last night.
"Is this yours?" I asked swaying it left and right.
"My name's Ted," he said really fast.
"Come to my house when it's dark."
We're friends now, me and Ted.
Plus, he's always there to tuck me into bed.

Hamdi Guled Hasan (9)
Wood Farm Primary School, Headington

My Candy Runaway!

There is a monster in the house!
He's green and furry.
His name is Fluffball!
Running down the hallway, he found the kitchen.
Opens the door, in he goes.
Going inside he finds a ladder,
He climbs up high and gets some candy.
"Run away, run away, I need to run away before someone captures me!"
He runs and he runs and the mouse gets scared.
He finds a place to hide.
He opens the box and eats a few.
A cat jumps up and screams, "Boo!"
"Run away, run away, I must run away!"
"Meow, meow, I will chase you! Meow, meow, meow!"
Tumble, stumble. "Whoops!
One scratch, two scratches! Ow!
At least I still have my candy!"

Narges Shafayi (9)
Wood Farm Primary School, Headington

My Family Life

Hello, I'm Huggle Monster,
I love hugs and love to giggle,
But sometimes I can be ungiggly
But whenever I'm happy I squeeze everyone
And flap around with my stripy sea-blue wings
And my colourful horns.

Whenever I'm unhappy I look at the swirly clouds
And when I begin to cry
I fly with the sparkling stars
And look at the bright moon.

When I start to feel happy again I go back home,
Get in my warm bed and I start my quiet snoring.
Monster Dog and I fall asleep.
Goodnight family, moon, stars and friends.
Out the lights go for the next day.
As I woke up I grinned with my blue tooth
And began on my adventures once again.

Shania Darcey Lewis (10)
Wood Farm Primary School, Headington

Echidna

Echidna, Echidna she lurks in a deep, dark cave.
From Greece comes Echidna who looks like a snake.
She has a human head and chest that's green and ever so rough,
She's such a horrid, ugly monster, no one enters her cave.

Many Greek heroes have tried to overcome her,
But she gave them such a fright, they turned their backs and ran away.

Echidna, Echidna she slithers around with her snake-like body.
You'd never want to see her as she is a true cannibal.
Her children are as ugly as herself.
They slither here and there.
You'd better keep away from them for they might call Echidna to catch you for their supper!

Senara Bambaravanage (10)
Wood Farm Primary School, Headington

The Day Moon Howls At The Wolf

I was lost. "Who's there? I'm so scared."
"Come get me, stop screaming," the voice said in glee.
A sharp snap.
"Ow, what was that? I feel the power running in my veins."
Fear was lost on a runaway train.
Suddenly ears sprouted from my head,
The headache kept going,
Time for bed.
Howl!
"That was strange," I mumbled as I woke up.
I was uncomfortable from the back,
My tail rose up,
"I'm a wolf, a werewolf.
Today I won't howl."
But the moon, the moon was humming,
As it howled, "Carry on moon, carry on."

Samrah Hirah Shah (11)
Wood Farm Primary School, Headington

Scruffy Fluffy Sall Is Out To Play

Scruffy Sall bumped down the shelf,
What a scruffy ball of fluff.
He went to his fluffer cookie treat
As fluffer cookies he loves to eat.
Down the stairs he tumbled,
"Hehehe," he mumbled.
Through the kitchen he tiptoed,
Up the shelves he climbed,
Past the oven and the window,
But he stopped and froze
As he saw that the sun out popped and morning came.
"Why is he here, who is to blame?"
Cried the owner of Sall,
"Who has moved my plush of fame?"
Where will Sall end up next?

Kacper Jakub Mackowski (9)
Wood Farm Primary School, Headington

Sweet Dreams

The seesaw creaked, no children around,
Then all of a sudden came a horrendous sound.
Sam was being chased by Annabelle,
She was holding a horn and it was ever so loud.

Sam ran away as fast as he could
But Annabelle was faster and grabbed him by the hood.
Her claw-like nails pulled out his hair,
She made sure he wasn't going anywhere.

Sam turned around and saw Annabelle's ghost-like face,
Sunken cheeks and bloodshot eyes,
The alarm went off and Sam woke up,
It was all a dream or a nightmare.

Cyrus Codrington Howard (9)
Wood Farm Primary School, Headington

Horned Night Giant

His eyes glow like lamps,
You can hear him at night as he stamps.

His scaly tail goes on for miles
And you can see his fangs when he smiles.

His huge, brown body is covered in fur
And his growl is as loud as a big tractor.

His fangs are as sharp as one million blades,
But when daytime comes he silently fades.

So watch out at night when he creeps around,
Stay under your covers so you can't be found.

Who knows who his next victim might be?
Maybe him, or her, or you, or me!

Stephana Sojan (9)
Wood Farm Primary School, Headington

Slendrina Returns

She's always hidden,
Watch out,
She will spook you out,
Make sure you don't look at her,
She's everywhere when you turn around,
She's quite a gale,
Find eight pieces to get out,
But there's more to find out.
Pictures on the walls will give you clues,
Bedroom picture is very familiar,
Even the keys can mean something.
Secrets to be found,
Follow the map to find your big secret,
Freedom is no use,
Much, much worse...
Be aware, is Slendrina still here?

Jannat Azam (9)
Wood Farm Primary School, Headington

Stinky Grible

In the deep forest, you can hear claws scratching the tree trunk.
It's Grible, the scary monster.
Be careful, he likes to eat children.
In the dark, you can see his bright red eye looking for food.
All the kids can feel the green fur in the wind.
Grible stinks like a cheesy, smelly sock you wear for weeks.
We can smell it from twenty miles away.
Run, watch out, stay under your cover, he is coming.
We nearly stand in slugs but we get away from him.

Oliver Cupi (9)
Wood Farm Primary School, Headington

Fofo Saves The Day

Mysterious days in Cruny Road, evil witchcraft appearing here and there,
A tall, slender, woman-like figure standing in the moonlight, flying when the sun comes out,
Its substantial teeth ready to chew on something gummy and juicy,
A little girl picked it up as a present for her mummy,
Fofo lit her mighty fire that crackled in the minute of silence,
One night the little girl woke up in a cramped space in horror.
"Fofo, what's wrong with you!"

Huda Boucetta (10)
Wood Farm Primary School, Headington

The Burping Monster

Be careful little children, he's out day and night.
He blends in with the trees right in front of your house
So always say pardon when you do a burp.
Bang! He comes out when you don't say pardon.
He is as colourful as a rainbow but as scary as a leopard.
He has legs that look like water slides
And horns that look like thorns
And a tummy with yellow different spots.
He is always sneaking up on kids when they don't say pardon!

Angela Soares Da Costa (10)
Wood Farm Primary School, Headington

The Goodnight Monster

When the lights are out and you're asleep
Make sure you don't make even a tiny peep
Because even if you're having a nice sweet dream
Beware, because you're about to have a frightening scream!
When he's having a giggle
Make sure you don't do a wiggle.
Also, don't ever open your eyes
Or else he'll say, "Come here, sweetie pie."
Instead, he'll do a tug on your hair.
OMG! What a nightmare!

Liana Roopesh (10)
Wood Farm Primary School, Headington

My Monster, Prickly

My monster's eyes, balls of fire,
It's like they are round black tyres.
My monster's fur is a soft sapphire sea,
When I cuddle him it fills me with glee.
My monster's claws are sharp, pointy needles,
When he cuts up paper, I feel so feeble.
My monster's teeth are spiked razors,
They cut absolutely anything like lasers!
Although Prickly seems like danger,
He really doesn't do anything major.

Adina Nadeem-Aftab (10)
Wood Farm Primary School, Headington

Slombie

Slombie, Slombie, why are you so slimy?
You try to be scary but you don't succeed.
Some people find you very, very frightening
But I find you cute indeed.
When people leave their food waste out you suddenly appear
But if their house is spick and span you better find a new career.
Slombie, Slombie, you're not so bad,
Your skin is kind of cool,
But if you stop this scaring act you'll definitely rule.

Gafar El-Hassan (10)
Wood Farm Primary School, Headington

Wyvern

W yvern, O Wyvern sure to give you a slight burn
Y ou shouldn't mess with Wyvern or else you'll be up in flames
V exed, well not at Wyvern, otherwise you'll be locked up
E lated, well Wyvern will turn that smile upside down
R idiculous Wyvern can't be beat, as long as Wyvern is around you'll be dead meat
N ever anger Wyvern, he'll rip you to shreds.

Kareem Osman (10)
Wood Farm Primary School, Headington

The Slime Beast Terror

The slime beast wakes up,
Goes to your room at midnight
And puts slithering slime all over you,
Then you wake up and see a hairy beast standing,
You scream with terror but it's no use,
The frightening monster puts slime in your mouth,
Then *bang! Bang! Bang!* the door opens.
I see a million monsters coming for me,
It's no use, I run, I am stranded...

Riannah Bonifuse (10)
Wood Farm Primary School, Headington

Story Of Fearnot

Down in a deep, dark alleyway,
There was a red and green dressed clown,
He jump scares a little girl called Sheldon.
Another day a little boy was walking across on the beach at night
And he jumps out again.
"Here I am," said Fearnot.
Carrying on at night, on the beach at 3:20pm,
Jump people over and over,
That was the worst that could ever happen to you.

Cora Destany Buron-Jackson (10)
Wood Farm Primary School, Headington

Earth Destroyer

I start in a factory,
I move around the world.
I ooze through the sea, rivers and wildlife.
The humans try to remove me,
Other humans keep making me.
I'm in every corner of the world
But they are slowly hunting me.
I'm considered rubbish wherever I go,
My greatest fear is that I'm no longer needed
And they will get rid of me...

Aimee Gardner Nott (9)
Wood Farm Primary School, Headington

Beware Of The Slugshot

Bored in bed, full of dread
Because of what my father said.
If you stay awake at night
You will get a big fright.
The Slugshot is wild,
Looking for a child,
I need to fall asleep
Before the monster starts to creep.
So I start counting sheep
Before it has a chance to leap
Into my cot.
So beware of the Slugshot.

Sofia Sarwar (10)
Wood Farm Primary School, Headington

My Beloved Monster

Do you know my monster
Who is called Ed?
He is always lying in my bed.

He has bright green eyes
And is giant in his size.
His orange teeth have a strange style
But they make me smile.
His blue fur is like a shaggy pillow.

I like him very much
And I'm not scared
When he gives me a touch.

Jette Wuerker (10)
Wood Farm Primary School, Headington

Rocky's Routine

All night, every night, he lurks around the house.
He sniffs and sniffs around the place for metal
things with his big, fat, hairy snout.
When he reaches the garage, with his sharp jaws,
Rocky munches on some metal saws
Without a crunch.
He saves some metal for tomorrow's lunch,
These monsters really are a crazy bunch.

Ayman Saadi Mahir (9)
Wood Farm Primary School, Headington

A Scary Monster Poem

My monster has eyes as round as a dinner plate,
It has sharp nails like a dagger,
Its mouth is dark and wide like a cave,
It has sharp teeth which are as pointed as needles,
Its hair is as long as a polar bear's hair,
Its body is as small as a balloon,
Its horns flick from side to side like it's an angry bull.

Hadia Haydari (9)
Wood Farm Primary School, Headington

The Return Of It

He will stalk you in the night,
Even when it's bright,
You won't be safe,
He won't be late
To kill you,
It doesn't matter who,
As long as you're a child
You might taste very mild,
So make sure you don't have any fears
Or your life might end in tears.

Daniella Drizi (9)
Wood Farm Primary School, Headington

The Unknown Monster

He comes in the night
Giving the children a fright.
The children shout with all their might,
Making sure there's no monster in sight.
The parents came,
The monster gets the blame.
He felt as ashamed as a cat who was caught drinking milk in pain
So he never came again.

Johana Jerish (10)
Wood Farm Primary School, Headington

The Stinky Monster

I see a monster
Underneath my bed.
He is yellow
And shy.

I see a monster
Underneath my bed.
He is short, smelly
And slimy.

I see a monster
Underneath my bed.
It's trying to attack me
But at the end is just
A little monster.

Nadine Da Silva (9)
Wood Farm Primary School, Headington

Laga Uga Maga

He came from the water
And he knows where you live
Don't get cheeky because he doesn't just sit.
He growls, he snarls, he lurks in the dark,
If he comes near beware of his farts.
Laga Uga Maga is his name,
Be careful because he doesn't want to play.

Aadam Waqar (10)
Wood Farm Primary School, Headington

Fragstein

He was as powerful as a lion,
But smart as Einstein.
He loved hunting for meat
As that was his favourite thing to eat.
Happily, he enjoyed building with wood
As he could.
He loved tricking people because it was so funny.

Ritish Balu (9)
Wood Farm Primary School, Headington

Glonpart The Monster

Glonpart thinks,
Glonpart stinks,
He likes to play,
He likes the day,
Sunny or not he still plays,
In or out he always has fun,
One way or another
He plays and plays
And still enjoys his day.

Yarai Georgeson-Campo (9)
Wood Farm Primary School, Headington

Mindtaker

Have you heard of the Mindtaker?
You haven't?
When you're walking on the street
Do not scream because he'll track you down
And never make yourself show...
Or you're dead!

Inaaya Bibi Asghar (10)
Wood Farm Primary School, Headington

Monster

Monsters are scary.
Monsters are green.
Monsters chase children
And make them scream!

Monsters are fluffy.
Monsters are red.
Monsters are ugly
And sleep under your bed!

Konnor Jordan-Madden (9)
Wood Farm Primary School, Headington

The Teddy Snatcher

I was in bed nearly asleep
When I heard a noise and decided to peep
Three large round eyes, pupils as small as flies,
Glaring at me, I froze with horror.
Nose as black as soot, same with his knees,
Teeth as sharp as a knife,
Sharpest thing I'd seen in my life,
Before I knew it, a big furry monster was stood in front of me
That's all I could see,
Tall and hairy, big and scary,
He looked really frightening, worse than lightning.
This was the Teddy Snatcher, the searcher,
He took people's teddies whilst they were babies,
A few days later, an envelope came
Saying he'd been lame and he was ashamed.
He said sorry,
He decided to throw a teddy picnic
To give people their teddies back,
He stole from them but in the end they all became friends.

Olivia Moore (9)
Woodlands CE Primary School, Woodlands

My Monster And Me

My monster comes out late at night
He used to give me such a fright
But really he is so soft
Though he lives inside my loft
When I should be fast asleep
Around the house I hear him creep
We like to read books and play with toys
Trying not to make any noise
Playing together is so much fun
It's a shame that I can't tell my mum
When we are hungry we like to snack
Then he gives me a piggyback
We then make sure we put everything away
To play again another day
Back in the loft he has to go
Where only I will ever know.

Lily Newton (10)
Woodlands CE Primary School, Woodlands

Monster Under Your Bed

Everyone said beware of the monster
Under your bed
Its teeth are like blades
But when it comes out to play
It wears cool shades.

Beware of the monster
Under your bed, they said
For its eyes are pits of darkness
But its heart is full of kindness.

Beware of the monster
Under your bed, everyone said
But they didn't know
It just wanted to be fed.

I've seen the monster
Under my bed, I said
It was sat in the dark
So we went to the park.

I'm friends with the monster
Under my bed
Its name is Fred.

Molly Holroyd (10)
Woodlands CE Primary School, Woodlands

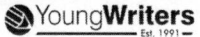

The Dwarf Monster

Deadly, small and unidentified,
The Dwarf Monster waits,
The Dwarf Monster hides,
Committing homicide to become satisfied,
Human blood motivates
The Dwarf Monster's genocide.
Underneath the floorboards, underneath the stairs,
You can't escape this creature,
He lurks in your nightmares,
Ripping you to pieces, ripping you to shreds,
This microscopic beast murders children in their beds,
He shows no remorse, he truly doesn't care,
So before you go to sleep, you'd better say your prayer.

Caylum Joseph Liu (10)
Woodlands CE Primary School, Woodlands

Beware Of The Whitiekins

Beware, beware, beware
Of the stare of the cat with the long black hair
If you dare to go outside at night
You might be in for a fright
She sits on skyscrapers as a queen would sit on a throne
Her evil eyes can turn you into stone
She rules the city from above
Why is it so much fun to scare the witches
When they fly by?
She steals sweets from kids on the streets
She strikes fear into everyone she meets.

Thea Stilgoe (10)
Woodlands CE Primary School, Woodlands

Horrid Borris

There was once a monster called Borris
He lived in a château with Dorris
Although they sound nice
They feast on live mice
And they grind up the bones like rice
They are miserable and spotty
And the château is dark and grotty
They would like you to stay
You would have to sleep in a barn
On the hay
Borris would like to meet you
But be careful, he might eat you.

Finlay Tempest (10)
Woodlands CE Primary School, Woodlands

Bogo Yo-Go

This is my monster
He's called Bogo
He is too scary
And he is a no-go
He's got ears like a donkey
And a tail that is wonky
He's purple and blue
He will scare you
He is really hairy and has no mouth
He's also a southerner, he's from down south
He is also quite naughty
And like my mum, he is a shorty.

Lilly Briscoe (9)
Woodlands CE Primary School, Woodlands

The Monster At The End Of The Wood

When I was five, I lived near a wood
My friends and I would go whenever we could
At night I looked outside my bedroom window
And there it stood.

Its face all white and eyes so bright
He only seemed to come at night
Nobody believed me, they said I was mad
Until the day it took my dad
From that day he never came back again.

Millie Wood (10)
Woodlands CE Primary School, Woodlands

Infinity And Beyond!

The crestfallen monster named Infinity
Travelled around space in his rocketship
Flying solo through the sky
Spotty, dotty all around
He had blood-red evil eyes
And hairy, scary horns
A cunning look within his eyes
And a repulsive smell following all around
Be aware of the giant snake-like venom!

Jack Oliver Kay (9)
Woodlands CE Primary School, Woodlands

The Scary Monsters

M onsters so big and scary
O ne so small, fuzzy and hairy
N ot a normal one, so small and cheeky
S ome monsters are also quite geeky
T errorising the neighbourhood
E scaping through the slimy mud
R emembering that they can be good.

Dexter George Fish (10)
Woodlands CE Primary School, Woodlands